# The Joy of Lex

### Life with a Service Dog

## John Thomas Clark

### With an Introduction by Dean Koontz

BLACK LAB BOOKS
Scarsdale, NY
www.BlackLabBooks.com

Copyright © John Thomas Clark

All rights reserved, including the right of reproduction in whole or in part in any form.
For permission, contact info@BlackLabBooks.com,
or P.O. Box 233H, Scarsdale, NY 10583.

Cover design and book design by Diane Buccheri
Front and back cover photographs by Keith A. Mancini

ISBN: 9780981946306

BLACK LAB BOOKS
P.O. Box 233H
Scarsdale, NY 10583

www.BlackLabBooks.com

For Ginny,
Christine and John
and,
of course,
Lex

With Love and Gratitude

# INTRODUCTION

I am not a master poet. Prose is my game. I am a frequent reader of poetry, however, and I am drawn to the work of Donald Justice, T. S. Eliot, Dryden, and others. You will never hear me presume to explain why any particular poem or poet is good. I only know what I like, and I very much like John Thomas Clark's sonnets about his assistance dog, Lex.

On the subject of dogs, however, I am better versed than I am in poetry. I have often written about dogs in novels and articles. In my faith, there are differing opinions about whether these beautiful and loving creatures have immortal souls, but the Church allows for the possibility. I do not entertain that possibility: I embrace with *certainty* the conviction that dogs have souls. We and our canine companions are souls in transit from one life to another, and we share a destiny.

Those dogs bred and raised and trained by Canine Companions for Independence, as was Lex, are exceptional creatures. A friend of ours, disabled by a spinal injury and confined to a wheelchair, had such a singular and wonderful relationship with his first assistance dog (now passed away) that he has said, given the choice of never having been disabled or never having known that dog, he would choose the dog and therefore the disability. This says more about the human-dog bond than anything I could write on the subject in a lifetime of writing.

My wife, Gerda, and I have been blessed with two dogs released from the CCI program. When we lost the first, Trixie, we felt as if we had lost a child, and the grief was deep and lasting. The second, Anna, is only two and a half as I write this, and her joy in every small detail of life sometimes brings tears of happiness to my eyes.

In this collection of sonnets, John Thomas Clark captures perfectly the details of his life with an assistance dog, relishes the beauty of small moments, and celebrates the grace that waits for us in every moment of the day if only we will open our eyes and our hearts to the recognition of it.

— Dean Koontz, 2008

A portion of the proceeds from this book will be donated to
Canine Companions for Independence.

# FOREWARD

I am a person who delights in his creature comforts. This book concerns those comforts. *The Joy of Lex: Life with a Service Dog* is dedicated to the delight of my life — Ginny, my bride of forty years, and to my daughter Christine and my son John. It is also dedicated to, and is all about, another delight — a four-footed one — Lex, my black Lab service dog, with whom I've been teamed for three years.

*The Joy of Lex* began with a suggestion from Ginny's brother-in-law Ray Powell, DVM, who thought an assistance dog might be of help with the Activities of Daily Living of my disabled condition. With Ginny's encouragement, we applied for admittance to the organization Ray suggested — Canine Companions for Independence (CCI). After a long and thorough vetting, we were accepted into their program at Medford, Long Island, where we were in training for two weeks in August of 2005.

In *The Joy of Lex*, you will meet Lex and accompany us through CCI's training program. Then, you will see us experience life at home and watch us interact with the outside world. These poems reveal how Lex works and how he plays, and demonstrate Lexie's marvelous personality. You'll observe an exceptionally smart dog (he knows his left from his right better than I do) as he performs many services for me — services he was trained to do such as picking up items I've dropped, opening doors and turning lights on and off. You'll also see him perform tasks he wasn't trained to do as when he saves me from certain injury in a serious wheelchair mishap. You'll even watch this intelligent dog question the choice of a New York Yankees relief pitcher, and though muse for these poems, you'll see him fall asleep as I read them to him**.** I hope he's a better judge of pitchers than poetry.

As my muse, Lex has enabled me to finally find and write about a positive dimension of my disability. That positive dynamic is Lex himself. For Ginny, my family and me, Lex is a joy to know, to have, and to hold.

In acknowledging the dramatis personae involved in this production, I must first announce my heartfelt thanks to CCI for having matched me with Lex, a beautiful dog who has improved my life in countless ways. I am indebted to Dean Koontz, not only for writing such a wonderful Introduction to *The Joy of Lex: Life with a Service Dog*, but also for all he and his wife, Gerda, do to make us aware of, and appreciate, the special relationships we can have with Man's Best Friend. To Derek Mahon, my former teacher, I am especially obligated to express my profound appreciation for his enthusiastic encouragement of my poetry and his thoughtful comments about this book. Eve Anthony Hanninen, editor of *The Centrifugal Eye*, leaves me greatly obliged for her most incisive thinking in evening out my poems. Diane Buccheri, publisher of *OCEAN Magazine*, has my enormous gratitude for the beautiful cover design and her marvelous layout of the book. A special and enduring tribute is reserved for the efforts of Keith Mancini for capturing the many faces and facets of Lex in his photographs. His love for his own chocolate Lab, Henna, shines through his work. I am beholden to my friend Richard Leonard who has provided valuable insights and helpful suggestions on every dynamic of this book from the very beginning.

Also, indispensable to *The Joy of Lex* has been my family. While Ginny and Lex have been center stage as the main characters, behind the scenes, Christine and John have worked tirelessly on this project since its inception, and their help has been incalculable in staging its presentation.

— John Thomas Clark

# PUBLICATION ACKNOWLEDGMENTS

A WORKHORSE OF A DIFFERENT COLOR, *The Linnet's Wings*, April 2008
AN AERIE FEELING, *Boston Literary Magazine*, March 2007
BLACK GOLD, *Tiger's Eye*, Autumn 2007
BLACK LIGHTS, *The Centrifugal Eye*, May 2008
BOWLED OVER, *Tiger's Eye*, Autumn 2007
DOG-GONE, *Boston Literary Magazine*, Summer 2007
JAZZED UP, *joyful!*, September 2008
LAP DANCE, *Contemporary Rhyme*, Spring 2007
MEASURED STEPS, *Leafpond*, April 2008
MY MORNING PICK-ME-UP, *Lucid Dreams*, August 2008
NEW WORLD NAVIGATORS, *OCEAN Magazine*, Fall 2008
OFF THE WALL, *The Storyteller*, December 2008
POETICS, *Contemporary Rhyme*, Summer 2007
POETRY AFFICIONADO?, *Innisfree Poetry Journal*, March 2007
SATURDAY, *The Healing Muse*, October 2008
SMOOTH SAILING, *Mobius*, 25th Anniversary Edition, 2007
SUPER DAY, SUPER DOG, *The Clockwise Cat*, August 2007
SUSPENDED ANIMATION, *Tiger's Eye*, Autumn 2007
TONGUE LASHING, *joyful!*, September 2008
UPS & DOWNS, *Mobius*, 25th Anniversary Edition, 2007
WEAPONS OF MASS DISTRACTION, *The Clockwise Cat*, December 2007
WONDERS, *Tiger's Eye*, Autumn 2007

# TABLE OF CONTENTS

| | |
|---|---|
| 15 | GOING TO THE DOGS |
| 17 | TROUBLES |
| 19 | FIRST DAYS |
| 21 | A MONUMENTAL TASK |
| 23 | A COMMAND PERFORMANCE |
| 25 | LAP DANCE |
| 27 | RUG DOGS |
| 29 | JAZZED UP |
| 31 | WEAPONS OF MASS DISTRACTION |
| 33 | ABRACADABRA |
| 35 | A ROSE BY ANY OTHER NAME |
| 37 | GAME, SET AND A WONDERFUL MATCH |
| 39 | THE DOG FROM "L" |
| 41 | TO TOUCH THE DIVINE |
| 43 | WONDERS |
| 45 | LEXIE STEPS UP TO THE PLATE |
| 47 | GRADUATION DAY |
| 49 | NEW WORLD NAVIGATORS |
| 51 | AN AERIE FEELING |
| 53 | TONGUE LASHING |
| 55 | SMOOTH SAILING |
| 57 | MY MORNING PICK-ME-UP |
| 59 | POETICS |
| 61 | MEASURED STEPS |
| 63 | STICK WORK |
| 65 | BLACK GOLD |
| 67 | A-MUSING |

| | |
|---|---|
| 69 | POETRY AFFICIONADO? |
| 71 | CONNECTED |
| 73 | A WORKHORSE OF A DIFFERENT COLOR |
| 75 | REMOTE POSSIBILITIES |
| 77 | DAN'S BEST FRIENDS |
| 79 | SUSPENDED ANIMATION |
| 81 | ON GUARD |
| 83 | THE MASTERPIECE |
| 85 | THANKSGIVING CENTERPIECES |
| 87 | BOWLED OVER |
| 89 | RABBITING |
| 91 | THE MAD DASH |
| 93 | DOG-GONE |
| 95 | BLACK LIGHTS |
| 97 | AN EARLY CHRISTMAS PRESENT |
| 99 | HE KNOCKS MY SOCKS OFF |
| 101 | OFF THE WALL |
| 103 | UPS & DOWNS |
| 105 | A NEW YEAR |
| 107 | SUPER DAY, SUPER DOG |
| 109 | SATURDAY |
| 111 | HAVING A BALL |
| 113 | DOUBLES, ANYONE? |
| 115 | ANIMAL MAGNETISM |
| 117 | BLIND CHANCE |
| 119 | MORE THAN LIP SERVICE |
| 121 | THE BLACK ROSE |
| 123 | NEW WORLD WAGTAIL |
| 125 | THE POWER OF THREE |

# The Joy of Lex

## GOING TO THE DOGS

I hope I'm not barking up the wrong tree,

but my family and my friends dogged me

to apply for a canine companion

with an eye to bridge the growing canyon

between me and things I'd do. So I asked

for a service dog. He'll be multi-tasked;

he can bring me the phone, open a door,

pick up anything I drop on the floor,

tow my chair when we go out for a spin —

these dogs enrich our lives. For this shut-in,

the pooch and I will make quite a team,

but what breed of dog will fulfill my dream?

A Lab? A retriever? A chow-chow? A

shot at the Iditarod with Team Chihuahua?

## TROUBLES

Four months late, and at the eleventh hour,

near the end of July, my new power

wheelchair finally arrived. In two days

I had to learn the chair's intricate ways,

then try to steer this state-of-the-art rig

up the ramp into the van for our gig

at Medford*. Easier said than done,

and, later that week, in my one-on-one

with a live Lex, I still lacked full command

of the chair. His look said, "I understand,"

as I committed mistake on mistake —

saying "Heel" for "Side" and then "Give" for "Shake."

His next look said, "I'll make you forget your troubles" —

he nosed into the water bowl and blew some bubbles.

*Medford — a Long Island, New York Canine Companions for Independence training facility

# The Joy of Lex

# FIRST DAYS

I stand in front of the room. The hostile

crowd is arrayed like isle after small isle

of angry rock in a river — blued bile

cataracts standing in my first wet mile

as a neophyte teacher. File on file

of flinty-faced sixth-graders, who revile

school, sit on my command. Inside I smile —

I'll survive the course down our ten-month Nile.

I sit in front of the room. The docile

creature stands before me. Almost servile

in his wish to please, Lex sits, stands, heels while

I give commands. That day, this versatile

dog, to this day, in his earned blue vest and collar,

listens as well as my best sixth-grade scholar.

# The Joy of Lex

## A MONUMENTAL TASK
for Jonathan Gerber, CCI Puppy Raiser

Michelangelo sees, says of a block

of Carrara marble, "Inside that rock

waits a statue." Wielding chisel, hammer

in his response to its inner clamor

for release, he roughhews to the soulshape

of his quarry. He foments its escape,

caressing the matrix to create a

masterpiece — a David or Pieta.

Kudos to the Angelas and Michaels —

the Johnnies-come-firstly in the cycles

of CCI dogs' lives. They take the pulp

of the dogs, mold it, shape it, to insculp

Dog Stars who help us navigate. First stargazers,

they are our serious, dedicated puppy-raisers.

# The Joy of Lex

## A COMMAND PERFORMANCE

One day, after our mid-morning break —

a romp for Lex in the exercise yard,

a cuppa and some oaten coffee cake

for us — back at Command Central, hard

at work are we eight. In this nerve center,

each of us — stationed at the apogee

of a large ellipse around our mentor —

pilots his dog. This is no cup of tea

when it's our turn. From the back of my throat,

I try a "Down" command. But a raspy sound

greets Lex. I gasp. I cough. And then the oat

flakes dislodge. Lex tilts his head. My voice found,

I give the command in my stentorian best

and Lexie does my "Down —" *and so do the rest.*

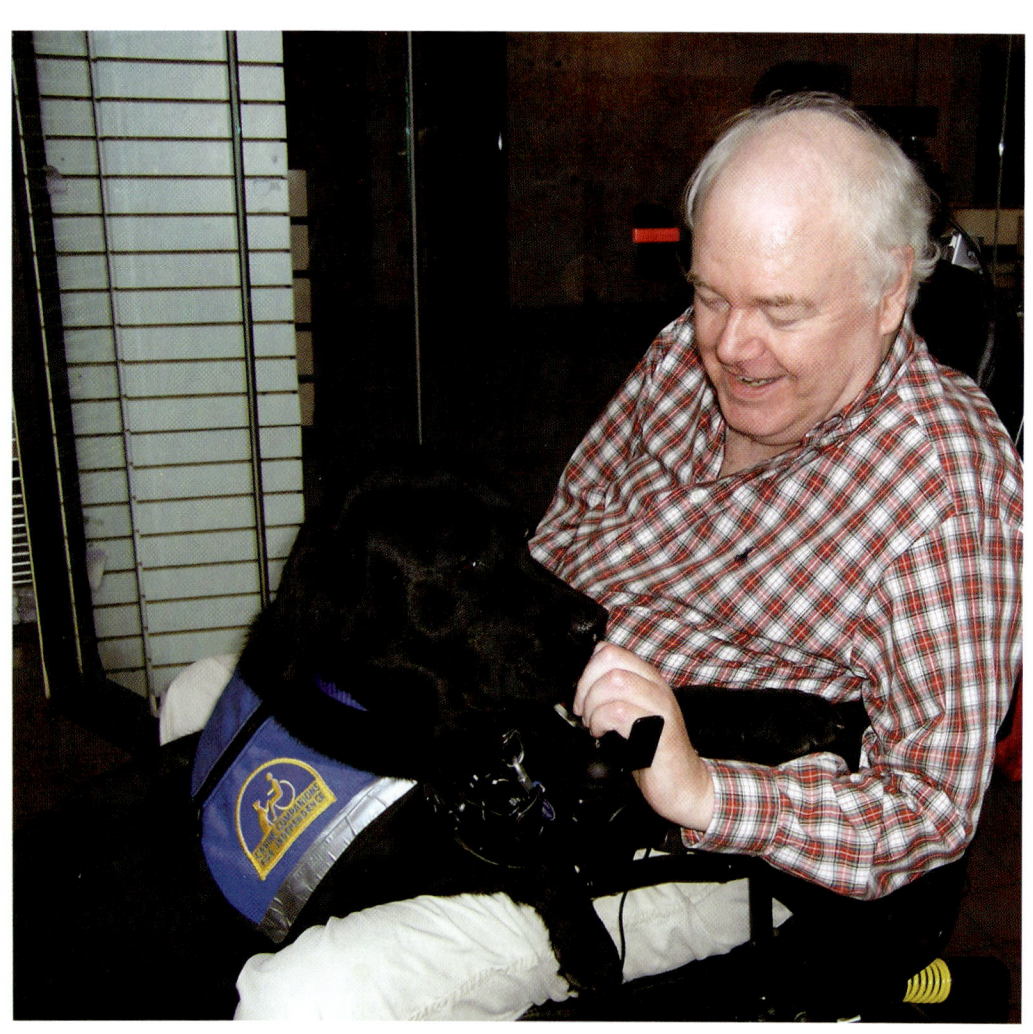

# LAP DANCE

Long gone were the days of the jitterbug

when our Sixties college crowd cut a rug

at some mixer. For us it was the twist,

the hustle, the stroll — gone now, in the mist

of time. On very different campus grounds,

eons later, instructors make the rounds

of my class. In a gym-like room, we're fanned

out with our partners for the "Lap" command.

I forget, leave the wheelchair in first gear,

and with my "Lap" call, Lex lands and we veer

left with his lean on my hand. His two-leg stance

drives us further left. For our slow, round dance,

I thank Lexie, amid my classmates' cheers,

for my first spin on a dance floor in thirty years.

# The Joy of Lex

# RUG DOGS

At our first Medford meet, there was Shaggy,

a reserved dog, not the wiggly-waggy

kind a Lab can be. His rough-piled, taupe coat

was nicely accented from tail to throat

with shiny, silver duct tape. A wood log

in truth, rug-wrapped, Shag was called Carpet Dog —

while we honed skills of control and command

you heard, "Carpet Dog, Sit." "Carpet Dog, Stand."

At home, LexMeister, lord of our nether

world, welcomes you to our carpet. Whether

you are there to do a crossword puzzle,

wrap a gift, stretch out, that paw or nuzzle

or body lean is for you. When he's at your side,

life with our Lexie is a magic carpet ride.

# The Joy of Lex

## JAZZED UP

We were tuning up our vocal technique

at school. I asked sweet-tempered Lex to "Speak,"

and he sang. When I said, in a whisper,

"Speak," he crooned. Next, my voice a bit crisper,

I said "Lap." Up he bounced. On my "Off, Sit,"

he sat down. But as soon as Lexie hit

the floor, I said "Lap, Speak." I heard my pup

purl the most dulcet tones when he came up.

While there was no change in his soft, sweet eyes,

his silky ears, revealing his surprise,

tilted. My improv — a woofy bebop —

had Lex join me for a doggy doo-wop.

Though not up to Mel Tormé, The Velvet Fog,

I can howl at those riffs with my velvet dog.

## WEAPONS OF MASS DISTRACTION
for Laura Ann Dubecky, CCI Graduate Program Cordinator

At CCI, teachers want to be sure

the dog doesn't succumb to any lure

while he works. Instructors try every ploy —

they scatter kibble, squeeze a squeaker toy —

to distract the dog. They call out his name,

roll him a ball, wave a stick for a game,

or they'll greet him in some spooky get-up,

or follow you home to do some set-up.

As we left our van, a flying feline

raced across the street. Making a beeline

for us was this wide-eyed, flabby tabby,

screeching. The bored look from my black Labby,

as the cat high-tailed for the back of our lot,

said, "Is that the best that CCI's got?"

# The Joy of Lex

32

## ABRACADABRA

Following that feline fly-by of "Flabs,"

the subject of our pre-class confabs

is — we're off to mingle with the inhabs

of the outside world. CCI keeps tabs

on us at the market, but some staffer blabs

about one dog (still, the best dog) who nabs

a bait-food bite. Good-natured jibes and jabs

still ring as I drive up my flagstone slabs.

As Lex debarks from our van, something grabs

his eye. Approaching are two frisky Labs —

romping. Lex stiffens and flexes his abs,

and like magic these CCI collabs

settle down. They walk past in a controlled trot

as Lexie's look asks, "Was that their next best shot?"

# The Joy of Lex

# A ROSE BY ANY OTHER NAME

Lex did so well, I thought we were exempt;

I never thought CCI would attempt

another ambush at home. Yet they dreamt

up one more — one that would serve to preempt

the morning ease. Lex, out in the back yard,

found a black cat with a striped, white tail, hard

by the rear fence. But Lex was on his guard

for this cat and its unique calling card.

In this "close encounter of the third kind,"

this was a polecat — not one that purred mind

you. I whispered, "Back." Lexie concurred. Hind

legs backed up. Front ones. Mine too. Our furred find

watched us shrink. If you deem me or Lex a wuss,

what would you do in a nose-up with a wood puss?

# The Joy of Lex

## GAME, SET AND A WONDERFUL MATCH

The eight dogs are in the exercise yard

while we're on break from class. It isn't hard

to tell which is Lex. A seven-dog pack

runs and romps as one, racing up and back

the length of the place. With a yellow ball

in his mouth, Lex lopes to any and all

who just might be up for his kind of fun —

he asks, "Tennis Anyone? Anyone?"

At home my singles-minded svengali

continues his game of serve and volley

with drop-shots then nose-pushes. His next serve

is in someone's lap. With this kind of verve,

Lex picks up my dropped shots, and my dropped face —

to win in life's game, I'm set with Lex, my service ace.

*The Joy of Lex*

# THE DOG FROM "L"

Hercules' twelfth labor finds him hellbound

for Cerberus, guard of the realm of Hades,

the netherworld — the abode of the shades

of the dead in ancient Greece. The knellsound

of this three-headed, serpent-tailed hellhound

roars. In response, Hercules' soft voice wades

across the Lake of Woe. The dog's rage fades

with these first kind words; he submits, spellbound.

As we wade through the otherworld hellground

of our handicaps, day on day, life jades

us. But dogs help us cross these woeful lades;

Lincs, littermates, of my British Lhound*

Lex, selflessly labor for us. Our days leaven,

for these dogs are not from 'ell, but rather from 'eaven.

*British Lhound — All Labrador retrievers can be divided according to type as either American or British. All Canine Companions for Independence dogs from the same litter are given names which begin with the same letter.

*The Joy of Lex*

*Three Variations on Killer Whale, 1985* by Robert Davidson graces the grounds of Pepsico's Sculpture Gardens, Purchase, NY. Permission granted.

# TO TOUCH THE DIVINE

To know a thing's right sense, to Donn Dog-Head

the folk go. They chant through the wet bog bed,

to his sweat lodge. He dons the dog cloak. Drum

heads pulse. He is at one with the clan thrum

now. He ends his day-long thirst with the dram

of the All-Known — to flood, then burst the Dam

of Worlds. On all fours he crawls in, then down

for the sense of He-Who-Wears-The-Dog-Crown*.

I have no need to line up worlds to spin

as one, to pierce cell walls of a world skin,

step through to the totem. I know the sense

of it — sans the rite through that far-in fence.

All I need do is look at this dog of mine,

for to know Lexie is to touch the divine.

*In ancient times when a clan needed special information, their shaman would use various devices to put himself in an altered state where he could communicate with the clan's totemic animal to gain special knowledge. In this case, it's the Dog Clan sending their shaman, the Dog-Head, to meet with the clan's deity, He-Who-Wears-The-Dog-Crown.

*The Joy of Lex*

# WONDERS
for Ellen Torop, CCI Program Manager

Khufu commanded the Great Pyramid

built to house his royal red bier amid

hieroglyphed walls. For his afterlife

ADLs*, the Pharaoh's Chamber was rife

with earthly trappings — a Sun Boat, gold throne —

anything he might need. This immense stone

tomb forms, in pale limestone and red granite,

the most beautiful crypt on the planet.

For ADLs, my seventy-pound rock

is Lex, a live pyramid of skilled-block-

on-raised-block. Due to his raiser, trainer,

my life's graced by this wondrous retainer.

When one looks at a CCI dog, he sees a

monument more beautiful than those at Giza.

*ADLs — Activities of Daily Living

The Joy of Lex

# LEXIE STEPS UP TO THE PLATE

Canine Companions for Independence School

teamed me with Lex from their prodigious pool

of pups. Lexie was an excellent choice;

if he had objections, he failed to voice

them, but I'm never good at right from left

so Lexie must have thought me brain bereft,

confusing "Heel" and "Side." In the kennel,

late that first night, he must have said, "Ten'll

get you twenty kibble, my guy is worse

than yours." There were no takers, and that purse

of pellets went unpursued. So Lex said,

"I'll bet, though my guy's likely brain dead,

I'll get him through this with lots of patience and love" —

in two weeks, we were a fit like an old baseball glove.

*The Joy of Lex*

## GRADUATION DAY

In two weeks, we fit like an old baseball glove

and now, at school's end, I am in awe of

my service dog, what he does for me. More,

Lex has me thinking I can touch all four

again. Lou Gehrig downplayed his bad break,

said he'd a lot to live for. My life's jake,

quite lucky to have been asked to attend

Medford, luckier to have Lex befriend

me. Teamed with Lexie, I can bust the curve

balls of life, however they break. His verve

has me thinking he will be my proem

to hitting home runs again. This poem

might be one of them. And that's why I say

I feel like Larrupin' Lou on this day.

*The Joy of Lex*

# NEW WORLD NAVIGATORS

From Tralee in the Kingdom of Kerry*,

Brendan the Navigator would ferry,

in a skin boat of tanned oxhides, his monks

to the New World. Other craft — Chinese junks,

Tyre's cedar boats — said to have made the trip

left no ready proof. When Columbus took ship

to Galway for Brendan's abbey, Clonfert,

he sought the saint's book — used it to convert

others. Although the rest is history,

like Brendan and Columbus, the mystery

of uncharted waters lies dead ahead

for me. But, Lex, my new sea dog, will shed

my barnacles of uncertainty, lead the way —

what you'd expect of a dog born on Columbus Day.

*Kingdom of Kerry — "There are two kingdoms in this universe, the Kingdom of God and the Kingdom of Kerry." — an Irish saying, probably originating in County Kerry.

# The Joy of Lex

# AN AERIE FEELING

A flightless eagle, I live on the edge

of your world now. No longer can I soar

for I am not in high feather. No more

can I ride life's sunlit thermals. The wedge

between us widens. But I have a hedge —

Lex — who flies to me and nests on the floor

beneath my bedside cliff. My Labrador

there out of loyalty, his service-pledge

roost, at my legs, insures I do not fledge

on my own. He places himself before

me so I cannot fall. To underscore

this, when I am on my morningside ledge

and my bird dog lights by my bedside shelf,

my heart soars for this is something he taught himself.

*The Joy of Lex*

## TONGUE LASHING

By three quarters past the six o'clock hour,

watching the news, Lex and I finish our

breakfasts. The storm lathers Maine, maneuvers

back for New York. Lexie's sweep tongue hoovers

his bowl — a Lab thing — for that last bantam

bit. He gathers up by now mere phantom

flecks, so he takes his bowl to the kitchen

at the anchor's next-hour news pitch. In

returning, his switch tongue still runs riot,

loud licking flicks the air. A soft "Quiet,

my friend, I'd like to hear what's being said,"

and he keeps that swivel tongue in his head.

I lean down to whisper he remains in good grace

and he looks up at me and slathers my face.

# The Joy of Lex

## SMOOTH SAILING

Mornings, when I dock at the computer,

Lex berths alongside. Before the booter

button is pressed, I perform a shakedown

cruise with him. To offset any breakdown

in the mastership of my sailmate's skills,

we perform commands, in our daily drills,

to keep him shipshape. He merits a snack

for a well-done Heel, Side, Sit, Front and Back.

Now Lex came alongside one peep o' day,

a strange look on his face. It said, "Belay

your orders, Captain." But his Pavlov drip

said no mutineer would hijack the ship,

for so eager was he for his prandial pelf*

he began that day's sea trial all by himself.

*prandial pelf — a tasty treat

*The Joy of Lex*

## MY MORNING PICK-ME-UP

We're not sure if Gioacchino Rossini

preferred his caffeine like Honore Balzac,

fifty cups of the finest grind, all black,

daily. Did he like his cappuccini

with extra milk? Not likely. Espresso

was key. Up on coffee, he told Honore,

he'd need fifteen to twenty days to score

an opera. For me, to fluoresce so,

a four-footed firkin* of inky coffee

greets me each morn. The steely aroma,

the anima of Lex is the soma†

I need to write. I look in those toffee-

colored eyes and know worlds, formerly seen afar,

close up, through the heady brew of my café noir.

*firkin — a small barrel
†soma — an intoxicating beverage

*The Joy of Lex*

## POETICS

I think Edgar Allan Poe's Siamese,

who as Poe wrote, dug in on his shoulder,

was the architect behind his macabre

tales. I suspect Poe's cat is the forbear

of my chocolate point, Frank, a sure devil's

familiar. With Frank, malevolent spews

meet me. But, Lex, my benevolent muse,

greets me with his waggly-wiggle, revels

at the sight of me, prompts me to forswear

dactyls of dour design. His tail throb

deflects the melancholy, the moulder

of Poe. To sculpt a lofty iamb-frieze

I call not on Frank, the mephisto cat,

but upon Lexie, my upbeat aristocrat.

*The Joy of Lex*

## MEASURED STEPS

With my mouthstick, I misjudged the measure

of my docking station, hitting it square

on the black metal post. My displeasure

flamed when it fell into quick disrepair

on floor contact — the wooden base disgorged

the post. Its twists, turns, left Lex untroubled —

the sideways, karate kick-shaped post, forged

like that, was easy to grip. Lex doubled

his efforts, though, with the base. Like a sawed-

off pyramid, it sat there, its beveled

edges sloping upward. Lex raked and clawed

its topside surface. Then it bedeviled

him no more. He flipped it. He stabled it

in his teeth, and then on "Up, Drop," he tabled it.

*The Joy of Lex*

# STICK WORK

I lean my mouth-held typing stick forward,

and miss its cradle. When it falls floorward,

to retrieve it, I urge it with my left

foot over to my right. Once there, to heft

it, I leftheel the rubber tip. This squeeze

move then lifts the sixteen-inch shaft. I ease

my right shoe neath the raised bite-plate which drops

to my shoe crown. Next, a pincer-move props

the stick straight up. If lucky, I'll snag

the biteplate between my fingers. I drag

it up my leg, wrestle it to my mouth;

when successful, my day doesn't go south.

But now I say, "Lex, Get, Hold, Lap, Give." With Lexie,

dropped sticks no longer mean bouts of apoplexy.

*The Joy of Lex*

# BLACK GOLD

Keats' advice to "fill every rift with ore"

was so much slag — silver moons and golden

sunsets were not for me. The mother lode

for my meter was found in the dark earth

of James Mangan whose Poe-like poetic

provided the proper mold and matrix

to form and shape my verse. His cicatrix-

ladened life appealed to my noetic

needs; his melancholy moods helped to birth

my Manganese. Now, Lex tempers the mode

of my poems. To Lex I am beholden

for how he enables me and for more —

unearthing a plus to my disabled fettle —

himself — he gilds my moods with his rarest mettle.

*The Joy of Lex*

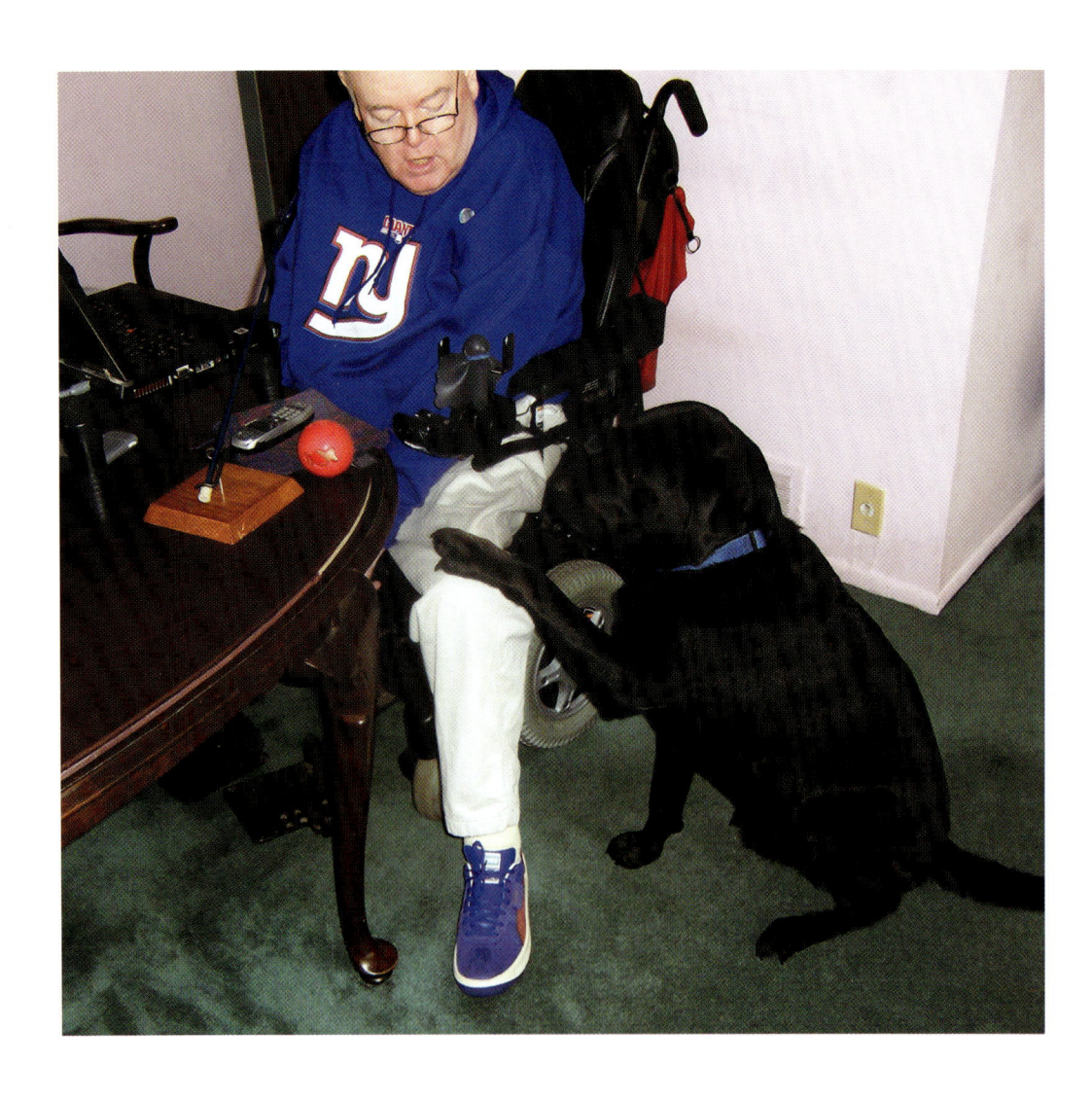

# A-MUSING

for Richard Leonard

In order to prime his poetic pump,

M. Balzac drank, with at least one lump,

maybe two, fifty jorums of java

each day, to coax his loquacious lava

to flow. Schiller's aromatic apple

would encourage his dactyls to dapple

the page. The close confines of a coffin,

for Dame Edith Sitwell, served to soften

word walls. Ben Franklin liked a tepid tub,

while Virginia Woolf joined a crowded club

of stand-up writers. A Wordsworth walk

was a tune-up for him to talk that talk.

For me, it is the touch of Lexie's aura;

it thrills up my senses and ignites my aurora.

The details of this poem were culled from an article published by the *New York Times* on November 12, 1989 by Diane Ackerman entitled *O Muse! You Do Make Things Difficult!*

# The Joy of Lex

# POETRY AFFICIONADO?

Novelist Osbert Sitwell understood

poetry to be like fish — if fresh, it was good,

he said. But if it was stale, it was bad,

and, he continued, if the poet had

no clue, the verser was advised to try

it on the cat. Now, Frank, our cat, will fly

at my approach, so who better to test

my rhymes on than the muse himself — the best

service dog. Nipper at the gramophone*

was Lex. On no finer house might I hone

my craft. And, yes, I did bring down that house;

for as I read, my sonnets served to douse

Lex, sphinx him. Next his head nestled on the floor,

his eyes flickered and closed and he began to snore.

*Nipper at the gramophone — the trademark for RCA Victor, a dog listening to his master's voice

# The Joy of Lex

# CONNECTED

for Ray Powell, DVM

From sagebrushed, rose-hued deserts in cactus,

to broken mesas, snowed peaks, his practice

safeguards all the land. Within the aura

of his aegis, the land heals. Fauna, flora

thrive. Rios grandes of Albuquerque

accolades gush forth for all the work he

devotes to wildlife — magically smitten

by Ray, a vet who's never been bitten.

Like the land, wildlife of New Mexico,

I owe Ray a debt for my Lexie, so

great a nexus to other worlds via

Lex do I have. It was Ray's idea —

a service dog — and with Lex, my home underwent

a magical change to a Land of Enchantment*.

*Land of Enchantment, the official nickname of New Mexico

Ray Powell is the former elected Land Commissioner of New Mexico (1993-2002). He currently works for Dr. Jane Goodall.

*The Joy of Lex*

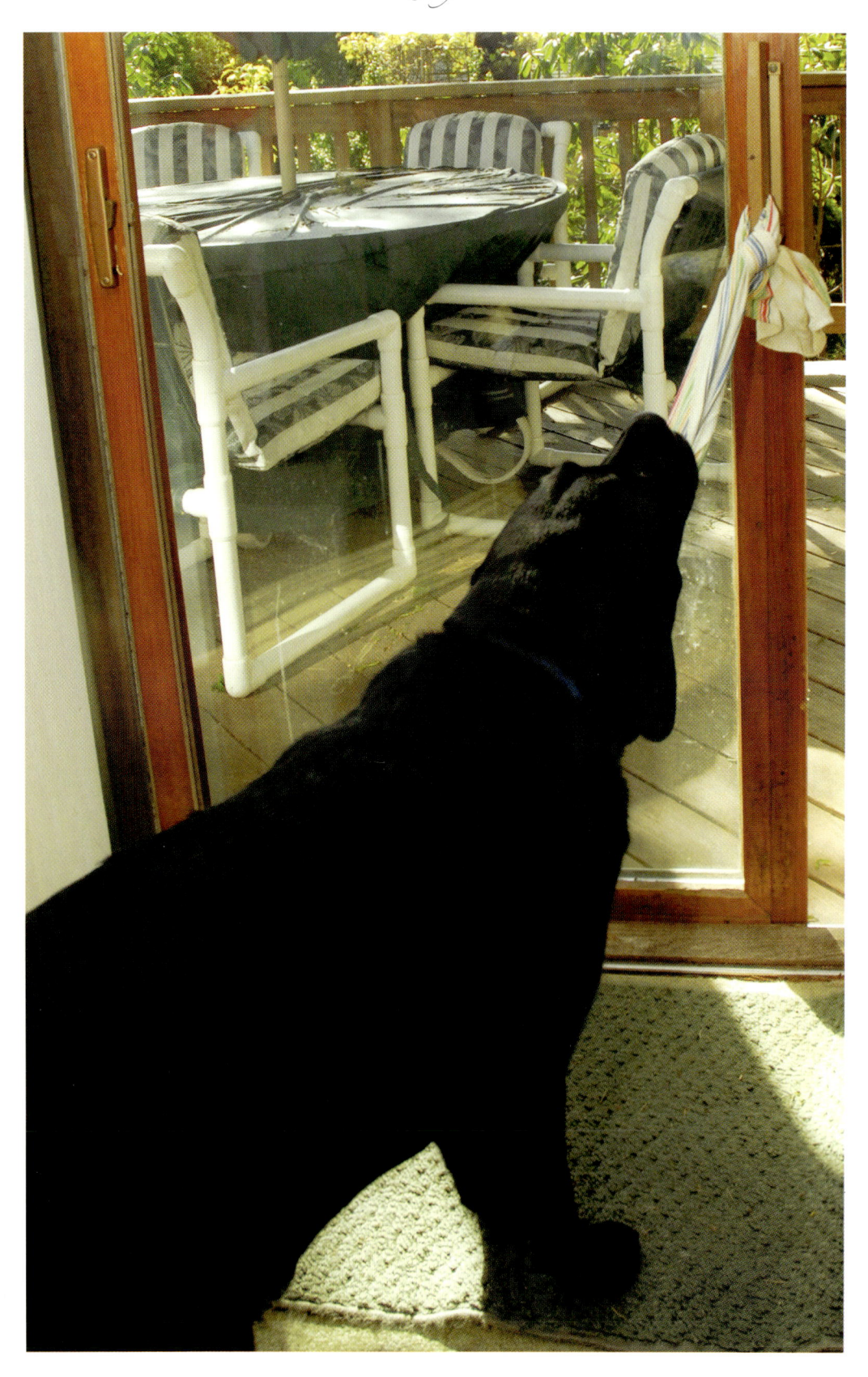

## A WORKHORSE OF A DIFFERENT COLOR

First bred in Lippiza, an Italian

town near Trieste, the Lippizan stallion,

though born black or some shade of sienna,

turns white in five years. At the Vienna

Spanish Riding School, while in a ménage

a deux with his rider, he learns dressage

and that famed, swaggering, high-stepping prance,

while Lex, in the pas de deux of my dance

macabre, eagerly heeds *my* prompts. The verve

of this black stallion in his quest to serve,

to retrieve my mouthstick dropped on the floor,

to tug off a sock, or open a door,

to pull a wash basket, turn on a light,

proves this paladin* with paws is my white knight.

*paladin — a heroic champion, paragon of chivalry

*The Joy of Lex*

# REMOTE POSSIBILITIES

Yankee Stadium stalwarts were in the thrall

of Chien-Ming Wang as he threw ground ball

after ground ball out against the Detroit

Tigers. If winning against his adroit

pitching was remote, less so was the chance

against Mo* in relief. The faithful's dance

in the aisles rocked the place with each mow down

and Yankee Stadium was renamed Mo-town.

But the screen blanked as the Yankees high-fived —

my remote fell. This setback was short-lived

though. Lexie pitched in without being told,

grasped the remote and tabled it. With this bold

relief pitcher in the shiny black coat,

possibilities for me are no longer remote.

*Mo — Mariano Rivera, arguably the best relief pitcher in baseball history

# The Joy of Lex

## DAN'S BEST FRIENDS
for Fred Waters and Dan O'Connell

From Cork, cold echoes of the banshee howl

rang. It was Dan, wrapped in an icy cowl

for Fred, his friend of fifty years. No more

would the crack* be mighty, the football score

matter, the pint taste the same for his boon

companion was wrenched away. All too soon

these foster brothers from a bygone age

were sundered, one at peace, one left in rage.

With call on call, sadness reigned but the week

Lex came home with us, I asked him to "Speak"

to Dan. Lex barked. Across the waves, Dan's hound

answered. The next three Speaks drew forth a round

in kind. And a laugh, then another from Dan

as he howled along with the best friends of man.

*crack — a good time (Irish slang)

*The Joy of Lex*

# SUSPENDED ANIMATION

The hard, green, golf ball-sized hickory nut,

down from the shagbark tree, lodged in the rut

there, on the walk, between the first two gray

flagstones, unseen. It refused to give way

to my power chair's ascent. A front wheel

slipped and slid. The chair spun left to heel

over a low stucco wall, where I found

myself affixed — three right wheels off the ground.


Although our team was less than a month old,

Lex sensed something wrong. Without being told,

he moved to my left. Dangling from the chair,

locked in, lockjawed and locked there, in mid-air,

I was awestruck as Lex ended my woes

by righting my chair — nudging it with his nose.

*The Joy of Lex*

## ON GUARD

From a mad encounter of the worst kind,

where my power wheelchair acts with a mind

of its own, Lex saves me. Out of one bind,

Lexie is not about to let me find

my way into another. His eyes clamp

me, their candlepower enough to lamp

our way in the darkest night or the damp

of a difficult day. His backward tramp

leads me. Up my inclined walkway we weave,

and with each step, Lex is on the qui vive*

for my unforward move. Still his eyes cleave

to me as we gain the top. As we leave

the ramp, and we're on my deck, then does the wax

of Lexie's eyes melt, then does Lexie start to relax.

*qui vive — on the alert

*The Joy of Lex*

## THE MASTERPIECE

for Laura "Matty" Matlock, CCI Trainer, who left her signature on Lex

In a Renaissance school, the old master,

to fulfill the demands of a vaster

patronage, oversees his apprentice

pool, piecing out tasks. Each will present his

skills — long laugh lines on an aquiline face,

four or five folds of intricate white lace,

green, rolling hills of a Tuscan landscape,

perhaps the spotted, gnarled, veiny handshape

of an old duke. Now, experts try to piece

together clues in paintings to release

the artisanship, for many a name

is dimmed within the confines of the frame.

But *my* four-footed masterpiece is best

recognized by his signature blue and yellow vest*.

*All Canine Companions for Independence service dogs must wear their vests when on duty.

*The Joy of Lex*

# THANKSGIVING CENTERPIECES

We are, to That Great-Vague-Something-Behind-

Everything-On-This-Planet*, grateful

for this country, grateful for the plenty

it yields. For the bounty on this table

we are thankful. We are, to the creature

who gave his all to be this centerpiece,

grateful — we hope it was a quick release

for you. For our newest family feature,

neath the groaning board — Lex — able

and ready to serve me four and twenty

hours a day, I give thanks. From our fateful

first encounter, no one needs to remind

me how my life is graced and centerpieced

by a dog who makes each day a Thanksgiving feast.

\*That Great-Vague-Something-Behind-Everything-On-This-Planet — novelist James Joyce's name for The Almighty.

# The Joy of Lex

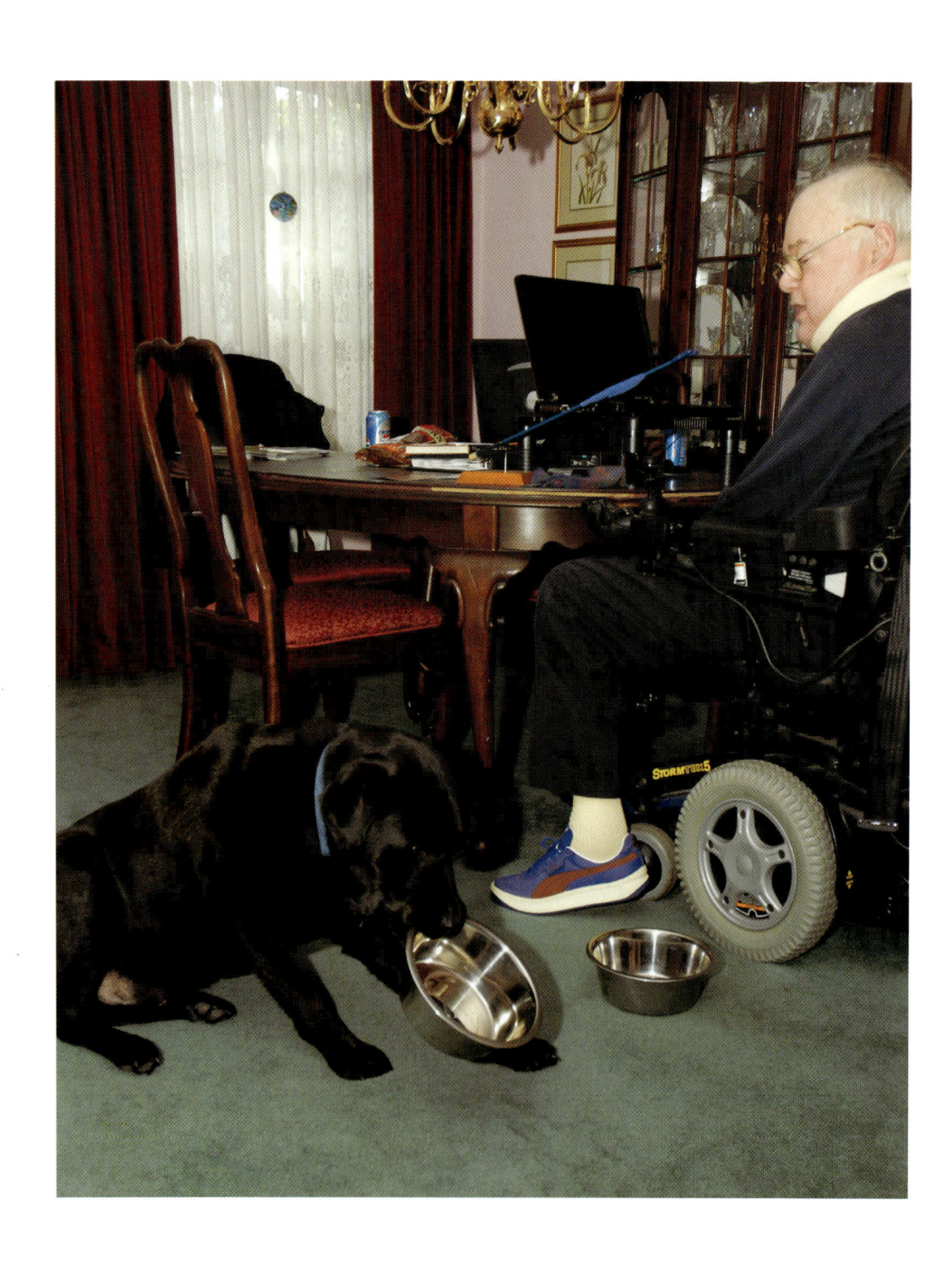

## BOWLED OVER

Mornings, sitting on the edge of the bed,

I breakfast and watch the news. Lex is fed

at the same time at my feet. When he's sated

(if that's possible) this clever-pated

pooch picks up his bowl without being told

and takes it to the kitchen. I was bowled

over — it took him just three days to learn

this. Evenings, when his gastric juices churn,

I say, "Lex, get your bowl." On its retrieve,

he dines with me. Hunger is his pet peeve,

though. Today, his inner dinner bell rang

early. Hearing the metal clink on fang

I said, "Too soon." But his hunger beckoned

so he put down his first bowl and brought me a second.

# The Joy of Lex

Life with a Service Dog

# RABBITING
for Joe O'Connell

My Dad called me "Wolf," a boyhood nickname —

after some book character? Whence it came,

who can say? For the speed with which I'd eat

supper, rabbit down to our South Bronx street,

to a stickball game, where I'd hope to drub

a "spaldeen*" three sewers†? He'd also dub

me "Doc" — I don't know why. It's a warm throw-

back to my youth, used just by cousin Joe.

Joe must have been heard by Lexiebubba,

for Lex does his doggy hubba hubba

when he sees an orange aperitif

between my lips — a baby carrot — chief

among his treats. Lex hares to me and his hock, hock,

hock says on my "Lap" command, "What's up, Doc?"

*spaldeen — a misspelling/mispronunciation for a pink Spalding rubber ball
†three sewers — roughly, the length of a New York City block

*The Joy of Lex*

## THE MAD DASH

Sometimes at the house, it's the aftermath

of energized walks that brings out the cub

in Lex. More often it's the afterbath,

though, that full body shake-out and the rub-

down that fuels him. He snatches at the towel,

has a chew, splays his front legs. His haunches

high, his head swivels left, right. His play growl

reports he's good to go. Then he launches

with head lowered and earflaps tight, to scud

through the living room. The coffee table,

ottoman, blue chair — with nary a thud,

he flies around them all. Then my sable-

coated comet, his third orbit complete,

comes back down to earth and lands at my feet.

The Joy of Lex

## DOG-GONE

Lex settles into the household routine

rather easily. From the beginning,

he takes an avid interest in the Yanks

and he demonstrates, during his third game,

how deep his grasp of pitching in relief

is. At the arrival of this rookie,

Lex hurls his last after-dinner cookie

treat with a gasp. Lex stares in disbelief;

his ears move forward as he hears the name

announced. He tilts his head. "No way he blanks

these guys," says Lexie's look. "The tenth inning

and tied? Use Mo*." So Lex woofs at the screen,

and at me, and goes to bed without being told

while, all by myself, I watch my Yankees fold.

*Mo — Mariano Rivera

*The Joy of Lex*

## BLACK LIGHTS

Callahan, the art teacher, drifted toward

the picture window, fingered the taut cord

there, while keeping up his end of the gab-

fest with his Friday night guests. His quick grab-

and-pull slammed shut the blinds. He mashed the switch:

lights doused. Click and hum. Purple rays pierced pitch

dark. *The Night Watch*\* emerged on the far wall

through the black light's glow and left us in thrall.

Empurpled days of my years-long night-watch-

wait dissipate with Lex. He serves to scotch

my darkness. Told, that for my bodily blues

there's no end-tunnel light, Lex-as-muse

lights up my life. And Lex will let *me* shine,

*oh* will he let me shine, this black light of mine.

\**The Night Watch* — a painting by Rembrandt

# The Joy of Lex

# AN EARLY CHRISTMAS PRESENT

On our first, not so foggy, Christmas Eve,

I glide back on our four months. I perceive —

as I smile at his wet, shiny, black nose

there, at my knee, as my love for him grows —

in Lex, I have a dasher. And a dancer,

a comet, a cupid and a prancer,

a dog, as clever as any vixen,

as I think back on, relive, that fix in

August. With blixem* speed, Lexie dunders†

to me, rights my chair before it sunders,

and me along with it. One walkway spill

avoided, he backs up my rampway hill

in front of me, his eyes fixed on me all the way;

Lexie can guide my sleigh, anytime, night or day.

\*blixem — lightning (Dutch)
†dunders — thunders from dunder (Dutch)

*The Joy of Lex*

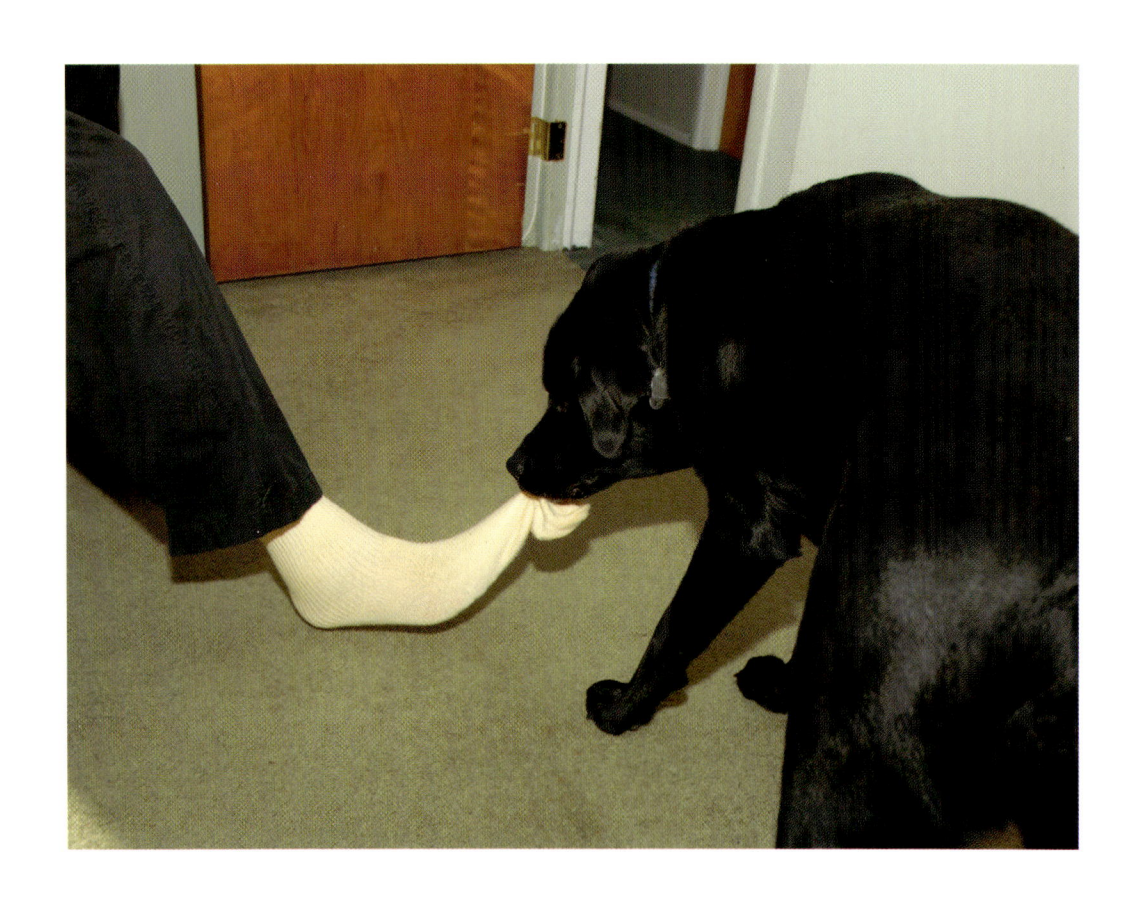

# HE KNOCKS MY SOCKS OFF

At the long day's end, it's time for bed

and Lex pitches in. He lowers his head

to grab his green blanket by my wheelchair

and remove it. With his usual flair,

Lexie grasps his quarry between his teeth

and backs up, tugging, tail wagging. Beneath

him, his captive follows. The path now clear,

I fire up the wheelchair, put it in gear,

roll off to the bedroom with Lex behind

me. But, in the morning it's tough to find

one sock. I ask "Lex, to where did you tug

it?" and that head tilt is his shoulder shrug.

Lex tugs roped doors, wash baskets, other things

and all day long, he tugs at my heartstrings.

*The Joy of Lex*

## OFF THE WALL

Lexie's bed is a foam, three-foot by four-

foot cushion which sprawls on our bedroom floor

when in use. When not utilized, it leans

on the wall near the two closets. This means

more traffic room during the day. In the first

three or four days with us, Lex was well-versed

in our nighttime routine. He watched and scoped

out the details, and, when told "Bed," he loped

to his floored sack and hit it. Understand

what Lexie now does on the "Bed" command,

floors *me*. By observing, he's learned to budge

that bunk by himself. With his shoulder nudge,

it moves from the wall, and, urged by his snout,

it's floored; he's aboard, and he's ready for lights out.

*The Joy of Lex*

## UPS & DOWNS

He's up for most everything — best of all

anything involving a tennis ball,

my Lex is. Also, he's up when I drop

something. He picks it up and the flip-flop

of his tail shows it — so eager to please

is he. On "Up" he'll rise to my arm, ease

out of my teeth the baby carrot treat

I hold for him. And he'll lie at my feet

unless he can climb up onto a throw,

or cushion on "Release." And there are no

downs, save when Lex gets it in his head,

as the down comforter slides off the bed,

in the middle of the night, and down to the floor

he ascends that comforter and it's mine no more.

*The Joy of Lex*

104

## A NEW YEAR

When my great-great-great grandfather died

March twenty-fifth, seventeen ninety-eight,

that was New Year's Day back then. While the date

for the Celtic New Year, down the long tide

of centuries, is unchanged, others like

Rosh Hashanah ebb and flow within one

month, year on year. Chinese New Year is done

the same way. This year, a serious spike

happed while reckoning the calendric cog

for the Chinese New Year. On this year's wheel,

February was breached, thrown off its keel,

when I boldly tugged The Year Of The Dog

back to last August. For then began my new year,

my new life with Lexie, my new reason for cheer.

*The Joy of Lex*

## SUPER DAY, SUPER DOG

Have you thought on an owner's nexus

to cats? At the behind-the-scenes plexus

of a show, with each puss primped for top shelf

blue ribbons, some think cats extend the self

and, in a pseudo-shamanic shape-shift,

will try everything short of a face-lift

to look like their cats — silvered crew cuts flare

to form oneness with the sterling shorthair.

Though dog folks can sport a totemic tress,

whose dogs emulate them? Amid the stress

of Super Day*, Lex, like me, gulps his food

and his drink, wears Giants Blue — and my mood

during the game. Big Blue doles out the final squelch —

in our win I cease wondering where Lex learned to belch.

*Super Day — Super Bowl Sunday

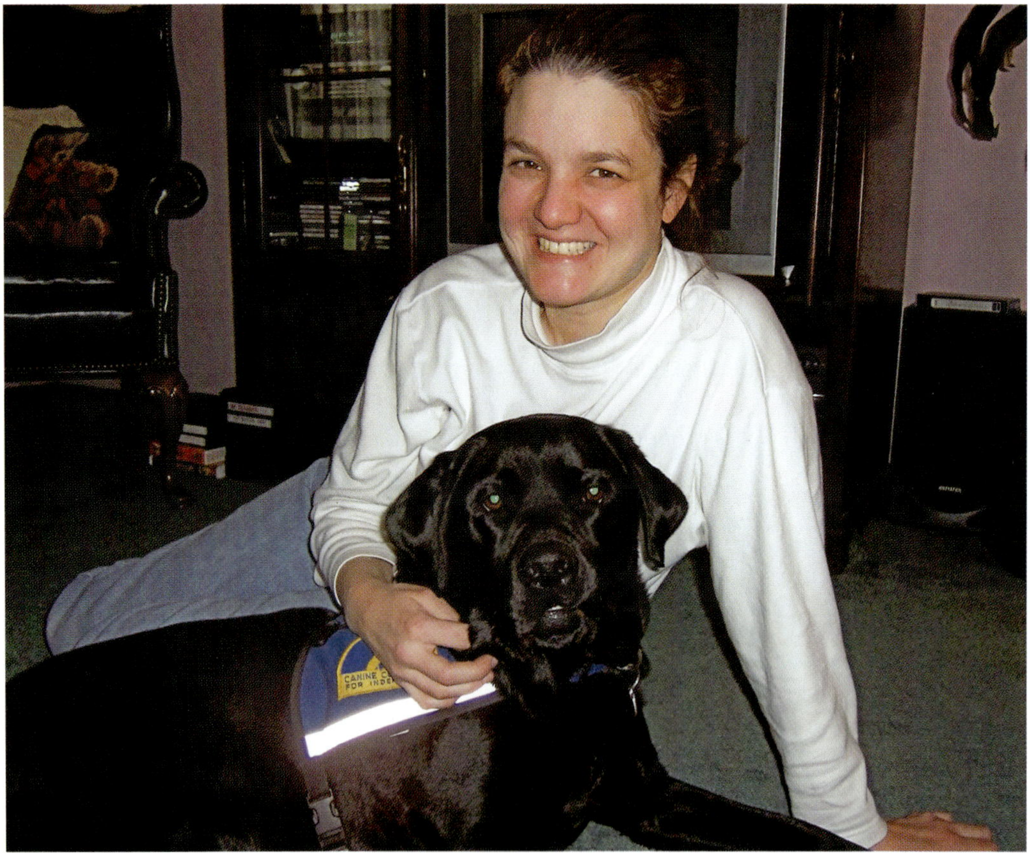

# SATURDAY

On Saturday, I drop my Yankee cap —

Lex retrieves it and puts it in my lap

with a soft "woof." I grin. Later, out for

a walk, Lex peers through a pale Labrador —

ignores his barked challenge. I beam. At home,

the rabbit blip on Lexie's radar dome

doesn't register, nor does the salute

from neighbor, Marty. I smile. Son John's brute

strength is a match for Lexie's on the rug

until John's grip eases. Lex yanks the tug

toy from his hand. I laugh. Lex wants to go

again and offers John the toy. I crow.

Chris said, "Dad, this dog has the magic touch,

because I've never seen you smile so much."

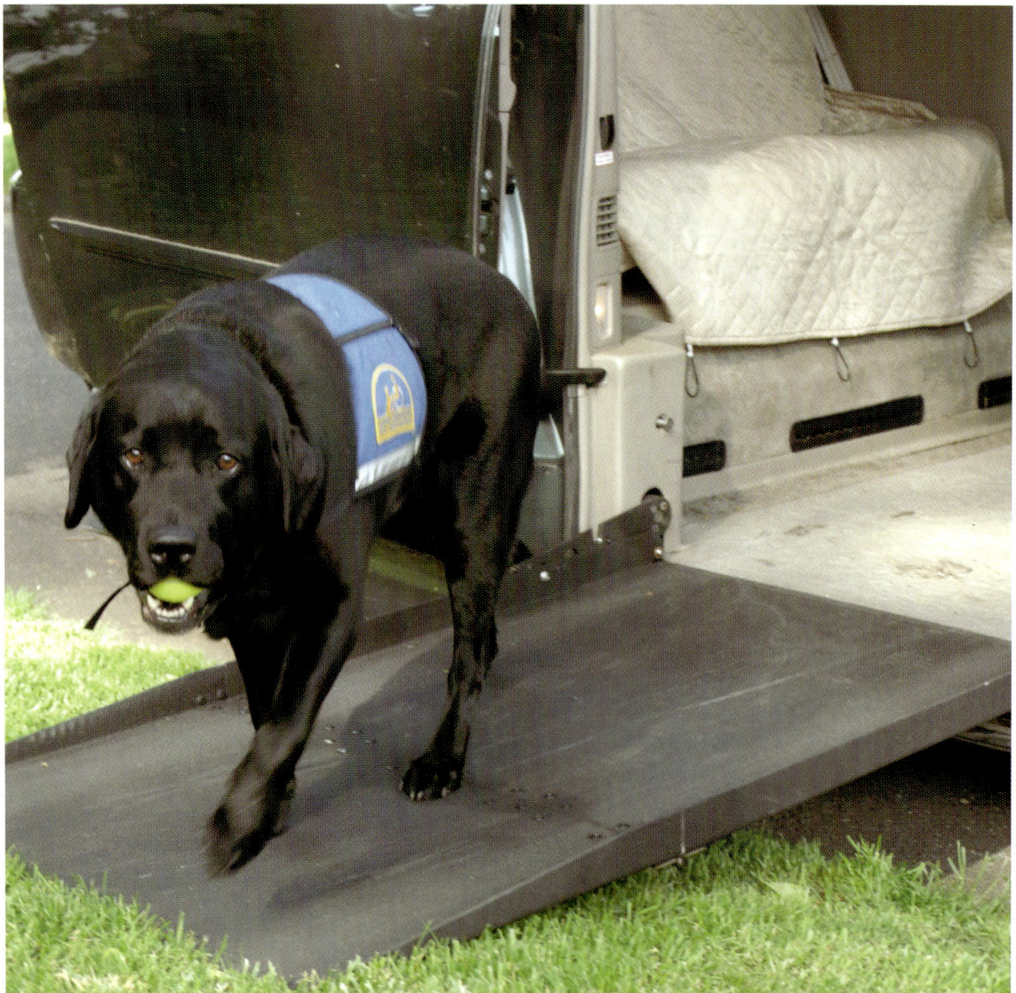

## HAVING A BALL
   for Tony Pizzuto

With Lex, we had taken two or three drives

to Tony's. On this drive day, September's

best, Lexie's gear, though snarled in a plastic

shopping bag on the floor, does not impede

my egress. Lexie's Lippizaner flounce

begins as Tony greets me. Off the ramp,

I see, hear Lexie anxious to decamp,

his eyes on Tony. Lex performs his bounce

down on command. On "Release" freed

to move on his own, with his third elastic,

stiff-legged, whirling jump, Lexie remembers

why Tony's fun. He darts up the ramp, dives

in his bag, past his Moocow, his food, past it all —

yes, past his food — desperate for his tennis ball.

# The Joy of Lex

## DOUBLES, ANYONE?
   for Bob Mautschke

For backyard barbeque access at Bob's,

from the brick path, Lex sees Bob set two leaves

from a dining room table before the wheels

of my power wheelchair. Doubling as ramps,

these wide, sturdy, interlocking boards slope

down from the two-inch, gray granite cobble-

stone trim. On the descent, not a wobble

haps. Seeing me safe, Lex is free to scope

out what's in Bob's hands and Lexie's headlamps

shine with double delight — tennis balls! Peals

of excitement erupt as Lex retrieves

one. "What if I throw two?" Bob asks and lobs

both. On Lex's return the crowd doubles up —

two yellow orbs glow from the mouth of my pup.

*The Joy of Lex*

## ANIMAL MAGNETISM

Maybe it's my sophisticated air,

the way I present myself — debonnaire,

sure of myself. Perhaps my savoir-faire

is the answer. Or the devil-may-care

style I exude in my suped-up hummer

of a wheelchair. In winter and summer,

women flock to me — a different drummer

for sure. Wait. What did that wag* say? Bummer!

I'm not the "handsome brute" — the chick magnet —

attracting them? The "he's so cute" dragnet

drawing them? The "gorgeous face," the wag bet,

was on my friend wearing the dog tag set.

Notwithstanding my self-indulgent coddle,

truly, it's Lexie who is the runway model.

*wag — a witty person

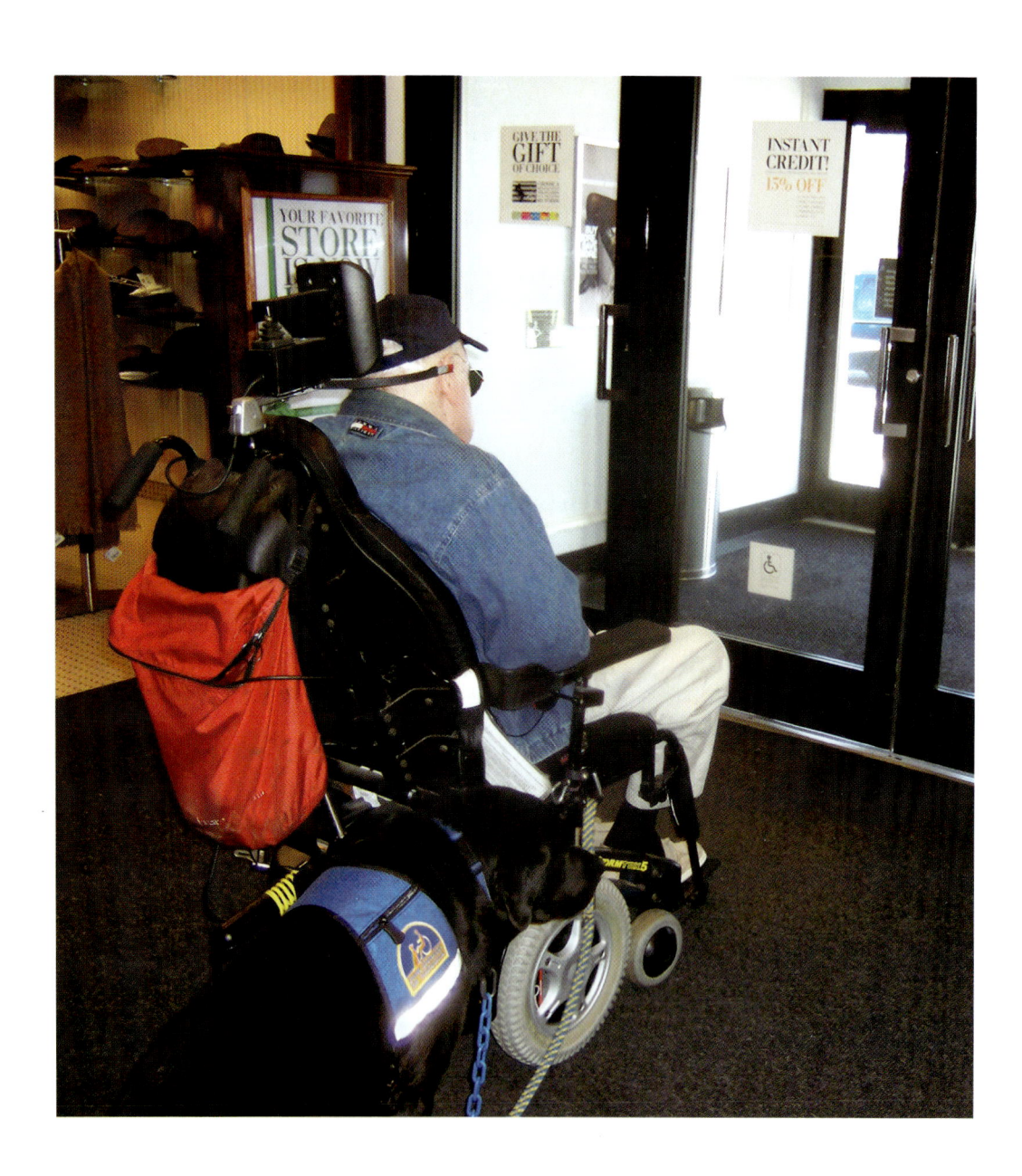

The Joy of Lex

# BLIND CHANCE

My first set of wheels was a white Mustang,

new, 'Sixty-six, red inside. Every year

I savored its high performance 'til fear

forced me to give it up. A blinding pang

of conscience said never again. No more

would I drive. The inexorable toll,

the slow, blind pursuit of total control

by the disease, was too much to ignore.

Now, I maneuver high-performance wheels

with my four-pawed pit crew through narrow aisles,

around mannequins, amid shoppers' smiles,

with not-quite-blinding speed. A woman squeals

at the cramped doorway as I give Lex a "Behind" —

"Get out of the man's way, that dog means he's blind."

*The Joy of Lex*

## MORE THAN LIP SERVICE

Sometimes folks ask "What is this Lexie, a

Lab? A Lab cross?" I tell them my sable-

coated teammate's a purebred Lab. They'll ask,

"Why does he wear that blue and yellow vest?"

and I'll reply, "It means he's on duty,

and no pet. He's a working service dog

who helps me." "What's he do?" I catalog

services performed by my black beauty

for me — "He'll open doors at my request,

turn on lights, carry bags." Perhaps the task

that's the best boon is the stuff of fable,

for he helped me lose my alexia*

for finding any relief from this disease —

I found it in this dog who's so eager to please.

*alexia — word blindness

*The Joy of Lex*

# THE BLACK ROSE

When you purchase that new car, your nexus

to it surrounds you in its new car-ness —

the clean smell, the gloss of burnished metal,

the sparkling engine — it takes forever

to wear off. But it does. And a new school,

a new house, a new neighborhood— all lose

luster in time. However, Lex, my muse,

is the shining exception to this rule —

this black flower won't lose his bloom. Never

will he fade, for each day's a new petal

as bright as our first one in harness

together. His efflorescence decks us,

our home with a beautiful bouquet

that is still new to me day after day.

The Joy of Lex

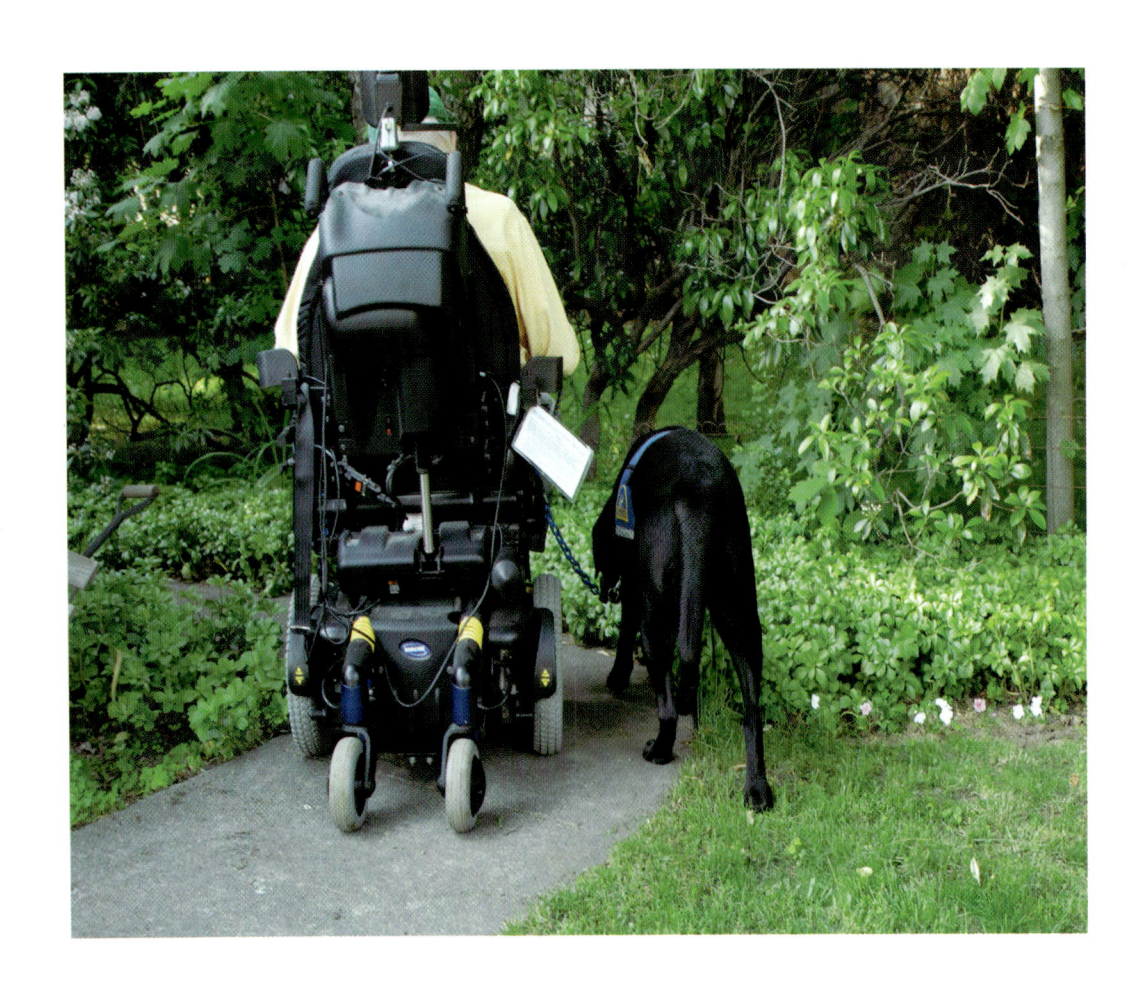

# NEW WORLD WAGTAIL

It is a small, Old World bird, the wagtail

is — smaller than our robin, it is sparrow-

sized, more slender of body and narrow

of end, an end which copies the flag tail

our mockingbird waves. Guess it's a balance

thing. The tails of the dawn chorus bob north

to south. Yet in my new world, back and forth

flies my wagtail's end. When through the valance

of the morning he breaks with bowl in teeth,

tail side to side, curtains for the night's sleep

it is — at small cost, though. Lexie's tailsweep

brushes aside all woes and weeds to wreath

my way down the garden path, appending

to each day the uplift of his happy ending.

*The Joy of Lex*

## THE POWER OF THREE

Well the ancient Irish knew the threeness

of things. Their gods and goddesses had three

aspects — Brigid was goddess of healing,

poetry and smithcraft. A three of threes

was special to them — a fleet of nine sails,

a group of nine maids, a herd of nine deer,

the onrush from a nine-charioteer

band in the pages of their early tales

heralded some mystical event. These

past three years I have known that feeling —

a power of three. It's empowered *me* —

and been the energy for my egress

to the outside world. It's my ebon-furred

Labrador, my service dog, my Lexie the Third.

# PHOTOGRAPHIC ACKNOWLEDGMENTS

Photographs by Keith A. Mancini pages 14, 28, 30, 36, 42, 44, 54, 56, 58, 60, 64, 72, 74, 76, 78, 84, 86, 90, 92, 94, 98, 100, 102, 106, 110, 114, 118, 122, front and back cover

Photographs by Virginia M. Clark pages 16, 18, 22, 24, 26, 32, 34, 38, 40, 46, 48, 50, 52, 62, 66, 68, 80, 82, 88, 96, 104, 108, 112, 116, 120, 124

Photographs by Jonathan Gerber page 20

Photograph by Jean Civikly-Powell page 70

# ABOUT THE AUTHOR

John Thomas Clark has had over 120 poems published in more than forty distinguished journals. Preferring to write in sonnet form, he enjoys its challenge — recounting a moment or telling a story with a beginning, a middle, a twist and an end, rhyming it, all within fourteen lines.

He lives in Westchester County, NY with his wife Ginny, his daughter Chris and Lex who knows it's playtime when his son John visits.

# FUTURE TITLES FROM BLACK LAB BOOKS

*The Joy of Lex II*

*Bronx Cheers* (poems of the Bronx)

*Mostly Munch* (poems resonating the art of Edvard Munch)

*Othering* (poems of change)

*The Chronicles of Saint Patrick* (a novel set in fifth-century Ireland)

BLACK LAB BOOKS
P.O. Box 233H
Scarsdale, NY 10583

www.BlackLabBooks.com